SOUNDS O.K.

TONY WALSH

Folens
Publishers

Editor: Deirdre Whelan

Illustrator: Lynn Loftus

© 1990 Folens Limited.
Albert House, Apex Business Centre, Boscombe Road, Dunstable, LU5 4RL.

Reprinted 1996.

Printed in Singapore by Craft Print

ISBN 1 85276099-0

Contents

Introduction

The purpose of this book is to continue and extend the work in Phonics and Spelling begun in Book 1, so that children may be equipped with the skill necessary for meaningful reading and to enable them to write rapidly and correctly whatever they wish to communicate to others. Children vary in their ability to do this and drill and practice are essential for all of them if learning phonic skills is to reach a stage of being almost automatic. To do this, it is necessary for them to have a knowledge of certain phonic combinations, such as vowel digraphs (two vowels making <u>one</u> sound), consonant blends and consonant digraphs. It is even more important that these sounds be put together smoothly and quickly so that they recognise words accurately and make some attempt to write words they have not met before.

A graded systematic approach to the teaching of phonics is essential if these aims are to be met. This book endeavours to do that.

At all times children should be encouraged to spell new words for themselves. If the word is mis-spelled it should be discussed and corrected and every effort should be made to classify the word in a family group which has a similar spelling pattern. Words combined in structures, are more easily recalled.

The spellings to be learned are carefully graded to ensure steady and substantial progress. The carefully selected sentences which may be used as an exercise in dictation provide ample scope for revision and reinforcement of work done.

<u>It should be noted that this book need not be confined to being used in one class only.</u> It may be used with any class the teacher deems appropriate.

Throughout the book when reference is made to letter *names* they are written like 'sk'.

Sounds of letters or groups of letter sounds are written like $\boxed{sk}$.

Short vowel sounds are written like $\boxed{a}$ $\boxed{e}$ $\boxed{o}$ $\boxed{u}$ $\boxed{i}$.

Long vowel sounds are written like $\boxed{\bar{a}}$ $\boxed{\bar{e}}$ $\boxed{\bar{o}}$ $\boxed{\bar{u}}$ $\boxed{\bar{i}}$.

st

| st | Practise the consonants **s** and **t** separately before blending them.

Try to think of as many words as you can that begin with | st |.

Then practise the builders.

sta

Box 1

| stab |
| stag |
| stand |
| star |

ste

Box 2

| step |
| stem |
| stench |
| stern |

sto

Box 3

| stop |
| stopper |
| stock |
| stocking |

stu

Box 4

| stub |
| stud |
| studded |
| stun |

sti

Box 5

| stick |
| still |
| stir |
| stirred |

st Practise the consonants **s** and **t** separately before blending them.

Think of as many words as you can that begin with **st**.

sta	ste	sto	stu	sti
Box 6	Box 7	Box 8	Box 9	Box 10
stake	steep	stoke	stuck	stitch
stale	steel	stole	study	stiff
state	steer	stove	sturdy	stilts
stable	steed	store	stuff	stile

In Box 6 silent **e** gives **a** its own name $\bar{a}$.

You remember from Book 1 that **ee** make a long $\bar{e}$ sound (Box 7).

In Box 8 silent **e** gives **o** its own name $\bar{o}$.

In Box 10 silent **e** gives the **i** in the word 'stile' its own name $\bar{i}$.

st *at the end of a word.*

Box 11	Box 12	Box 13	Box 14	Box 15
fast	pest	lost	dust	list
mast	nest	cost	rust	fist
last	rest	frost	must	mist
past	test		just	whist

sp

| **sp** | Practise the consonants **s** and **p** separately before blending them. |

Now practise the builders.

spa	**spe**	**spo**	**spu**	**spi**
Box 1	Box 2	Box 3	Box 4	Box 5

spa	spe	spo	spu	spi
span	sped	spot	spud	spit
spanner	speck	spotted	spun	spin
spat	spell	sponsor	spur	spill
spatter	spend	spoke	spurt	spirit

Words ending in **sp** .

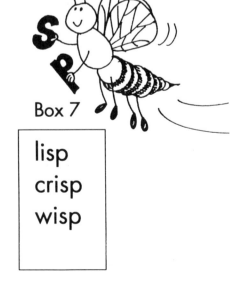

Box 6

hasp
rasp
gasp
clasp

Box 7

lisp
crisp
wisp

sm

| **sm** | Practise the consonants **s** and **m** separately before blending them. |

Then practise the builders.

sma

Box 1

> smash
> smashed
> smack

sme

Box 2

> smell
> smelt
> smelter

smo

Box 3

> smog
> smock
> smoke

smu

Box 4

> smut
> smug
> smuggle

smi

Box 5

> smith
> smirk
> smile

Silent **e** gives **o** in 'smoke' its own name $\boxed{\bar{o}}$.

Silent **e** gives **i** in 'smile' its own name $\boxed{\bar{i}}$.

Time for a test

1. The sick horse will spend the rest of the day in the stable.
2. The jacket was studded with stars.
3. The smith came into the store to buy a rasp.
4. My Dad fell over the stick and hurt his spine.
5. Stand on the step and stick the mast in that spot.
6. Did you smile when Pat spoke about the stench?
7. Get a spanner in the store to open the stiff clasp.
8. How much did the stove cost?
9. The smell of the stale crisps made me sick.
10. When I stoke the fire the smut falls out.

A further test can be done by writing your *own* sentence for some of the words you have learned.

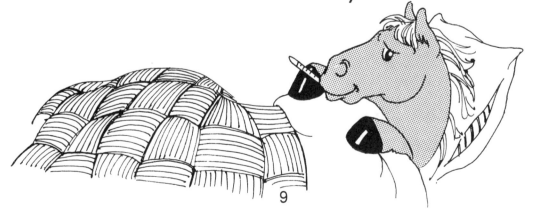

sn

sn	Practise the consonants **s** and **n** separately before blending them.

Then practise the builders.

sna

Box 1

snap
snag
snack

sne

Box 2

sn**ee**ze
sn**ee**r

sno

Box 3

snob
snort
snore

snu

Box4

snug
snub
snuff

sni

Box 5

snip
snick
sniff

ee make an $\bar{e}$ sound.

Silent **e** gives **o** in 'snore' its own name $\bar{o}$.

SW

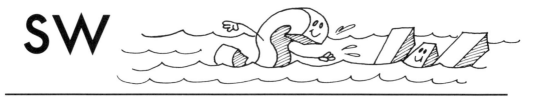

| **SW** | Practise the consonants **s** and **w** separately before blending them. |

Then practise the builders .

swa	**swe**	**swi**	**swi**
Box 1	Box 2	Box 3	Box 4
swam	swell	swim	swish
swag	swelter	swimmer	swill
swagger	sw**ee**p	switch	swig
	sw**ee**t	Swiss	swipe

ee make an $\boxed{\bar{e}}$ sound.

Silent **e** gives **i** in 'swipe' its own name $\boxed{\bar{i}}$.

In a number of words where **a** follows **w**, the **a** has an $\boxed{o}$ sound. In the following words the **a** has an $\boxed{o}$ sound.

swallow   swan   swap   swamp

sc   sk   sch

sc **sk** **sch** Each of these makes the sound **sk** .

SC

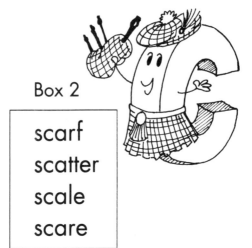

Box 1

scab
scar
scalp
scalpel

Box 2

scarf
scatter
scale
scare

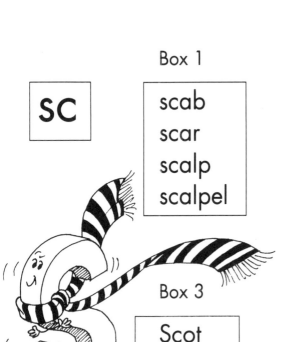

Box 3

Scot
scorch
score
scold

Box 4

scum
scut
scurry
scuff

sc   sk   sch

sk	Box 1	Box 2	Box 3	Box 4
	skate	skip	skill	skull
	skates	skin	skittles	skulk
	sketch	skid	skiff	skunk
	skeleton	skim	skirt	

Words ending in **sk**.

Box 5	Box 6	Box 7
task	rusk	disk
mask	dusk	risk
bask	tusk	frisk
cask	husk	brisk

sch

Box 8

school	scholar	scheme

13

str

str	Make sure you can blend these three letters together.

Practise the builders.

stra

Box 1

strap
strand
straddle

stre

Box 2

stretch
stress
str**ee**t

stro

Box 3

strong
stroke
stroked

stru

Box 4

struck
strut
strum

stri

Box 5

strip
string
strike

ee make an $\bar{e}$ sound.

Silent **e** in 'stroke' gives **o** its own name $\bar{o}$.

Silent **e** in 'strike' gives **i** its own name $\bar{i}$.

scr

scr These three letters will sound as **skr**.
Make sure you can blend them together.

Box 1

> scrap
> scrappy
> scrape

Box 2

> scram
> scratch
> scratched

Box 3

> scr**ee**ch
> scr**ee**n
> scroll

Box 4

> scrub
> scrubbing
> scruff

Box 5

> scribe
> scribble
> script

I'm sure you know now what silent **e** does in the words 'scrape' and 'scribe'. What about the **ee** in 'screech' and 'screen'?

spr　　　　spl

spr Make sure you can blend these three letters together.

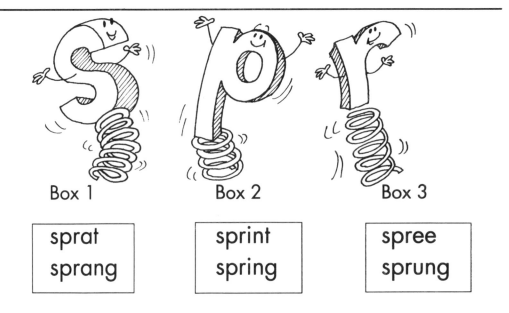

Box 1　　　Box 2　　　Box 3

| sprat | sprint | spree |
| sprang | spring | sprung |

spl Make sure you can blend these three letters together.

Box 4　　　Box 5

splash	split
splutter	splint
splendid	splinter

16

Time for a test

1. A splinter from the desk stuck in my skin.

2. It takes a lot of skill to skate well.

3. Did you scribble over the script on the scroll?

4. The cask fell with a splash into the lake.

5. We play skittles on the strand on Sundays.

6. If you stretch the strap it will split.

7. There is a scab on the scar on my scalp.

8. The swimmer had a snack after school.

9. If you snort the snuff it will make you sneeze.

10. The skunk will scurry into the street if the dog barks.

Soft C

In Book 1 you were told that **c** has a $\boxed{k}$ sound.

Now we are going to see that **c** will have the $\boxed{s}$ sound when the next letter in the word is **e**, **i** or **y**.

When **c** has the $\boxed{s}$ sound it is known as **soft c**.

Box 1

| ace |
| race |
| face |
| space |

Box 2

| ice |
| nice |
| mice |
| dice |

Box 3

| dance |
| chance |
| prance |
| glance |

Box 4

| cell |
| cent |
| centre |
| century |

Box 5

| fence |
| pence |
| force |
| since |

Soft C

Box 6

place
trace
grace
brace

Box 7

rice
slice
twice
price

Box 8

pencil
stencil
cancel
parcel

Box 9

city
circle
circus
decide

Box 10

office
fancy
cycle
cycling

What do you notice about the words 'circus' and 'cycling'?

Soft g

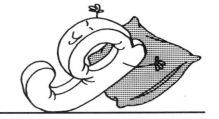

In Book 1 you learned the sound **g** made, in words like 'gap', 'get' and 'gate'. Now we see that **g** also makes another sound.

g usually says the sound of $\boxed{\textbf{j}}$ when the next letter in the word is **e**, **i** or **y**.

When **g** says the $\boxed{\textbf{j}}$ sound it is known as **soft g**.

Box 1

age
rage
page
cage

Box 2

range
change
grange
strange

Box 3

angel
danger
ranger
stranger

Box 4

large
barge
charge

Soft g

Box 5	Box 6	Box 7	Box 8
hinge	ridge	cabbage	college
singe	midge	savage	image
tinge	fridge	garage	gentle
fringe	bridge	village	sponge

What do you notice about the word 'garage'?

Exceptions to this rule

Box 9	Box 10	Box 11	Box 12
anger	give	tiger	giddy
hunger	gift	target	giggle
finger	girl	together	forget
linger	gear	begin	girder

Vowel sounds

In the following pages we will learn about the sound two vowels coming together make.

An easy way to remember groups of letters standing for the same sound is to colour code them like this –

Green	**ee** **ea** bee week tea seat **ee** and **ea** have the same sound as **ee** in green.
Gold	**oa** **ow** soap coat snow grow **oa** and **ow** have the same sound as **o** in Gold
Grey	**ai** **ay** tail rain day play **ai** and **ay** have the same sound as **ey** in Grey
Blue	**ue** **ew** **oo** true glue few blew cool moon **ue**, **ew** and **oo** have the same sound as **ue** in Blue.

Vowel sounds

White	**ie** **igh** **y**
	tie pie high might my reply **ie, igh** and **y** have the same sound as **i** in white.
Brown	**ou** **ow**
	house mouth town now **ou** and **ow** have the same sound as **ow** in Brown.
Fawn	**au** **aw** **all**
	haul because jaw lawn ball small **au aw** and **a** in 'all' have the same sound as **aw** in fawn.
Red	**ea**
	dead head Here **ea** has the same sound as the short **e** in Red.

Have you noticed that **ea** belongs to the Green code and also the Red code? Have you also noticed that **ow** belongs to the Gold code and the Brown code?

ee from the green code

From Book 1 you remember that **ee** together make an $\bar{e}$ sound.

Box 1
bee
see
fee
flee

Box 2
week
seek
meek
cheek

Box 3
feel
heel
peel
reel

Box 4
feet
meet
beet
sleet

Box 5
sweet
fleet
street
sheet

Box 6
feed
need
deed
heed

Box 7
speed
bleed
steed
greed

ee from the green code

In the words below the letters **ee** together make the $\bar{e}$ sound.

Box 8

peep
weep
keep
deep

Box 9

sweep
creep
sheep
sleep

Box 10

seen
been
green
queen

Box 11

beer
jeer
steer
cheer

Box 12

beef
reef
sneeze
breeze

Box 13

cheese
teeth
speech
beech

Box 14

thirteen
fourteen
fifteen
sixteen

Box 15

seventeen
eighteen
nineteen
between

ea from the green code

In the words below the letters **ea** together have an $\bar{e}$ sound.

Remember that:-
*When two vowels
go out walking,
the first one does
the talking.
(and usually says its own name).*

Box 1	Box 2	Box 3	Box 4
sea	eat	cheat	near
tea	seat	wheat	hear
pea	heat	treat	fear
flea	meat	pleat	tear

Box 5	Box 6	Box 7
year	lead	dream
dear	read	cream
spear	bead	steam
clear	plead	stream

ea from the green code

In the words below the letters **ea** together have an $\bar{e}$ sound.

Box 8

teach
reach
peach
preach

Box 9

heal
deal
seal
steal

Box 10

east
feast
beast
least

Box 11

leap
heap
reap
cheap

Box 12

peak
leak
weak
speak

Box 13

ease
tease
please
easy

Box 14

bean
lean
mean
clean

Box 15

season
reason
repeat
defeat

Words which sound the same

You must be sure of these words, because if the wrong one is used it changes the whole meaning of the sentence.

ee   ea

ee	ea
see	sea
week	weak
reel	real
meet	meat
leek	leak
reed	read
steel	steal
flee	flea
beech	beach
tee	tea

Time for a test

1. The spaceman went over the fence at great speed.
2. Every circle has a centre.
3. John will have a feast if he can reach the peach on the tree.
4. The garage was in the centre of the lovely village.
5. Who took the large slice of meat from the fridge?
6. When the ranger saw the beast he was in great danger.
7. A beech tree fell with great force last week.
8. The deep cut began to bleed but the cream will make it heal soon.
9. The steel pipe will leak so please keep back.
10. The sheep were seen on the green near the stream.

 **from the gold code**

Remember that the **o** is the vowel we will hear and it will say its own name $\boxed{\bar{o}}$.
a keeps quiet.

Box 1

oat
boat
goat
coat

Box 2

moat
float
stoat
throat

Box 3

coal
foal
goal
shoal

Box 4

oar
roar
soar
boar

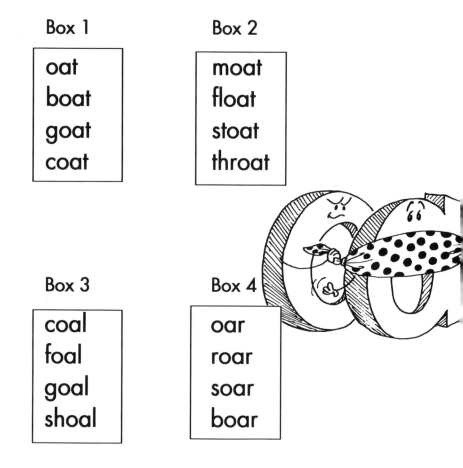

 **from the gold code**

Remember that the **o** is the vowel we will hear and it will say its own name $\bar{o}$.
a keeps quiet.

Box 5

> toast
> roast
> coast
> boast

Box 6

> loan
> moan
> roan
> groan

Box 7

> oak
> soak
> cloak
> croak

Box 8

> coach
> poach
> roach
> loaf

Box 9

> road
> load
> hoard
> board

from the gold code

In the words below the **ow** has the same sound as the **o** in **gold** – long $\bar{\text{o}}$.

Box 1

| low |
| row |
| sow |
| bow |

Box 2

| tow |
| grow |
| crow |
| throw |

Box 3

| glow |
| snow |
| flow |
| show |

Box 4

| blow |
| slow |
| stow |
| know |

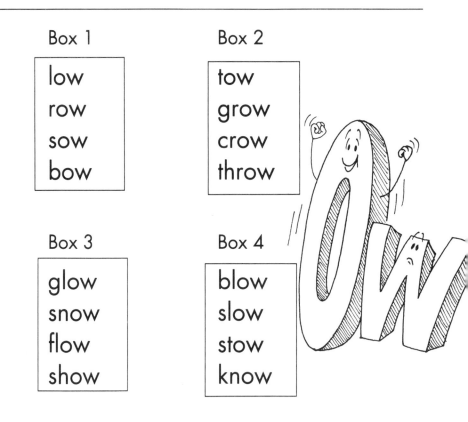

The **k** in the word **know** is silent.
You will learn about silent letters in Book 3.

 **from the gold code**

In the words below the **ow** has the same sound as the **o** in **gold** – long $\bar{o}$.

Box 1	Box 2	Box 3	Box 4
below	arrow	yellow	swallow
elbow	barrow	fellow	shallow
shadow	harrow	follow	widow
window	sparrow	hollow	tomorrow

Have you noticed that **ow** is at the <u>end</u> of all of these words?

Spelling Tip:

oa   ow When this sound comes at the <u>end</u> of a word it is usually spelled **ow**. When it comes in the <u>middle</u> of a word it is usually spelled **oa**.

Here are some words where **ow** has an $\bar{o}$ sound and is not at the end of the word.

Box 5   own   blown   grown   bowl   mower

ai **from the grey code**

Remember the first vowel is the sound we hear and it does the 'talking' or says its own name $\overline{a}$
The second vowel keeps quiet.

Box 1

| aid |
| maid |
| raid |
| afraid |

Box 2

| rail |
| mail |
| sail |
| snail |

Box 3

| pail |
| nail |
| jail |
| tail |

Box 4

| pain |
| main |
| rain |
| train |

Box 5

| brain |
| drain |
| grain |
| plain |

Box 6

| gain |
| stain |
| chain |
| strain |

ai from the grey code

Remember the first vowel is the sound we hear and it does the 'talking' or says its own name $\boxed{\bar{a}}$ The second vowel keeps quiet.

Box 7	Box 8	Box 9	Box 10
Spain	saint	aim	raise
slain	faint	claim	praise
sprain	paint	obtain	waist
again	faith	remain	sailor

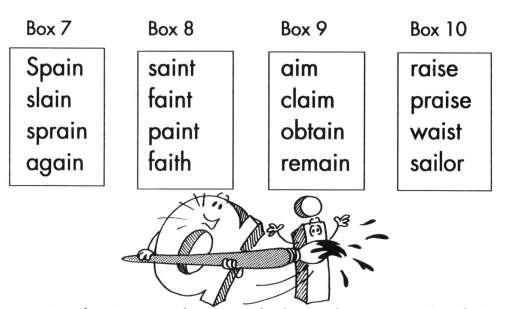

In Book 1 you learned that the sound of the vowel was changed a little when the vowel was followed by **r**.

Because **ai** has an $\boxed{\bar{a}}$ sound it will also be changed slightly when followed by **r**

Box 5 | hair   pair   fair   chair   stairs

ay from the grey code

In the words below the **ay** has the same sound as the **ey** in **grey** $\bar{a}$.

Box 1	Box 2	Box 3
day	pay	stay
hay	ray	sway
say	lay	play
may	way	tray

Spelling Tip: **ai ay**
When this sound comes at the <u>end</u> of a word it is usually spelled **ay**.
When it comes in the <u>middle</u> of a word it is usually spelled **ai**.

ay from the grey code

In the words below the **ay** has the same sound as the **ey** in **grey** $\boxed{\bar{a}}$.

Box 4

pray
fray
stray
spray

Box 5

clay
away
always
anyway

Box 6

delay
repay
display
betray

Box 7

today
yesterday
holiday
x-ray

Do you remember the spelling tip for **ai** and **ay**?

Time For a Test

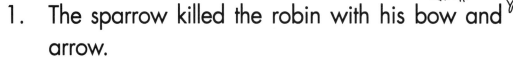

1. The sparrow killed the robin with his bow and arrow.
2. My mam let a roar when she saw the shadow of the goat at the window.
3. If you delay I'm afraid you will miss the train tomorrow.
4. The farmer uses a harrow to break up the clay.
5. The crows always eat the grain which falls on the road.
6. I had a pain in my throat and could not swallow.
7. The lorry went to tow the coach which broke down on the main road.
8. We see a great display of yellow and green flags.
9. The men in the boats saw a shoal of fish near the coast.
10. Remain at the board and raise your hand again.

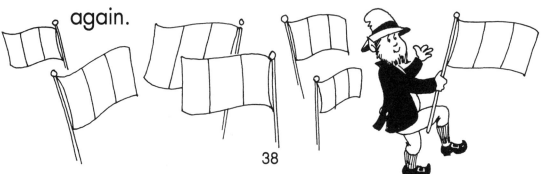

ue from the blue code

The **ue** in the words below sound the same as the **ue** in the word **blue**.

Box 1	Box 2	Box 3	Box 4
due	true	cue	avenue
blue	glue	rescue	statue
hue	flue	value	tissue
Sue	clue	argue	continue

If **ue** comes in the middle of a word, then the word is split into two syllables and the **u** will sound as long $\bar{\text{u}}$.

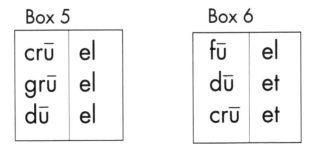

Box 5	
crū	el
grū	el
dū	el

Box 6	
fū	el
dū	et
crū	et

 **from the blue code**

In the words below the **ew** has the same sound as the **ue** in 'blue'.

Box 1

dew
few
new
pew

Box 2

stew
chew
view
knew

Box 3

flew
blew
drew
brew

The **k** in the word 'knew' is silent.

Box 4

crew
grew
screw
threw

Box 5

Jew
hew
yew
slew

Box 6

spew
strew
renew
nephew

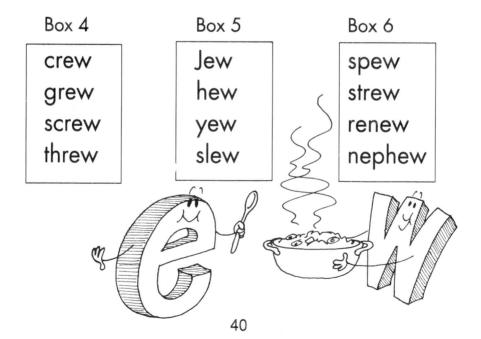

OO from the blue code

In the words below the **oo** has the same sound as the **ue** in 'blue'.

Some of the words have a short **oo** sound as in 'book' and 'look'.

Others have a long **oo** sound as in 'room' and 'roof'.

Box 1	Box 2	Box 3
good	cook	took
wood	hook	brook
hood	look	crook
	book	shook

Box 4	Box 5	Box 6	Box 7
hoot	root	cool	room
loot	shoot	fool	broom
boot	scooter	tool	gloom
coot	choose	pool	bloom

 **from the blue code**

Box 8	Box 9	Box 10
roof	moon	loop
hoof	noon	hoop
proof	soon	troop
spoof	spoon	stoop

In the following words the **oo** has a long $\bar{o}$ sound

door	floor

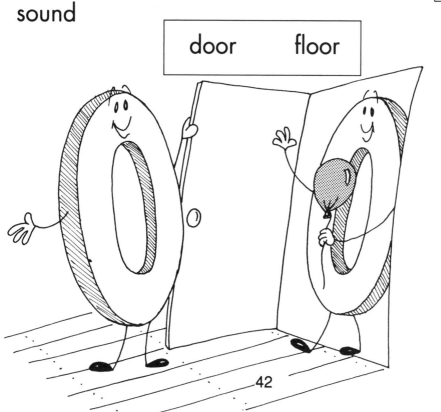

42

ie   igh   y

from the white code

---

ie has a long **ī** sound.

Box 1	Box 2	Box 3
pie	pies	cried
tie	ties	dried
lie	lies	fried
die	dies	tried

---

igh has a long **ī** sound.

Box 4	Box 5	Box 6	Box 7
high	might	right	slight
sigh	tight	sight	blight
thigh	night	bright	plight
nigh	fight	fright	flight

Box 8

light	lighter	delight

ie igh y

from the white code

y has a long **ī** sound.

Box 9	Box 10	Box 11
by	cry	sky
my	dry	sly
fly	fry	shy
why	try	spy

Box 12	Box 13
reply	tyre
occupy	type
satisfy	typist
multiply	typing

Time for a test

1. John's nephew blew the light out last night.
2. The new statue will occupy a spot on the avenue.
3. Sue tried with all her might to get out of the blue pool.
4. A high tree grew by the little brook.
5. How did the class in school know how to multiply?
6. The cruel king threw the cook in jail.
7. If you continue the duel someone must come to the rescue.
8. Glue might stick the screw in the broom.
9. The troop stood as soon as they saw the fight.
10. Who knew that the crew threw the crook into the sea?

OU from the brown code

In the words below the **ou** has the same sound as the **ow** in 'brown'.

Sometimes **ou** and **ow** are called the 'ouch' sounds.

Box 1

| house |
| mouse |
| blouse |
| trousers |

Box 2

| out |
| bout |
| lout |
| about |

Box 3

| stout |
| shout |
| spout |
| clout |

Box 4

| snout |
| trout |
| scout |
| sprout |

Box 5

| pound |
| round |
| sound |
| hound |

Box 6

| found |
| bound |
| mound |
| wound |

Spelling Tip: If the 'ouch' sound is in a word, the rule is in most cases it will be **ou** before **nd**, **nt**, **t**, **d**, **th** and **se**. Never **ou** at the end of a word.

OU from the brown code

In the words below the **ou** has the same sound as the **ow** in 'brown'.

Sometimes **ou** and **ow** are called the 'ouch' sounds.

Box 7

| ground |
| around |
| abound |
| aground |

Box 8

| loud |
| aloud |
| cloud |
| proud |

Box 9

| pouch |
| couch |
| slouch |
| voucher |

Box 10

| pounce |
| bounce |
| trounce |
| flounce |

Box 11

| our |
| flour |
| hour |
| sour |

Box 12

| mount |
| amount |
| mountain |
| fountain |

If the 'ouch' sound is in the word, what is the rule?

OW from the brown code

In the words below the **ow** has the same sound as the **ow** in 'brown'.

Box 1	Box 2	Box 3	Box 4
now	down	crown	owl
how	town	frown	fowl
cow	gown	brown	prowl
row	clown	drown	growl

Box 5	Box 6	Box 7	Box 8
howl	power	brow	jowl
towel	tower	crowd	scowl
vowel	flower	rowdy	allow
trowel	shower	powder	

au | from the fawn code

In the words below the **au** has the same sound as the **aw** in fawn.

Box 1

haul
Paul
maul
fault

Box 2

cause
because
pause
applause

Box 3

author
autumn
August
auction

Box 4

sauce
saucer
saucepan
sausages

Box 5

launch
laundry
daughter
Maud

Box 6

caught
taught
naughty
autograph

Spelling Tip:- **au aw**
When this sound comes in a word, in most cases the rule is
au before **nd**, **nt**, **t**, **d**, **th** and **se**.
Never **au** at the end of a word.

 **from the fawn code**

In the words below the **aw** has the same sound as the **aw** in 'fawn'.

Box 1
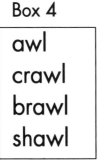

saw
paw
law
jaw

Box 2

raw
thaw
draw
straw

Box 3

lawn
yawn
dawn
prawn

Box 4

awl
crawl
brawl
shawl

Box 5

flaw
claw
outlaw
gnaw

Box 6

drawn
drawer
trawler
awful

 The **a** in 'all' has the same sound as the **aw** in 'fawn'.

Box 7

ball
fall
tall
wall

Box 8

call
hall
stall
small

50

Time for a test

1. My mam let a shout when she saw the mouse in our house.
2. Bounce the brown ball on the ground beside the lawn.
3. The tall clown fell into the fountain because his trousers fell down.
4. The outlaw was in a brawl in the town near the mountains.
5. Peter's daughter fried a pound of sausages in the saucepan.
6. August is the first month of autumn.
7. Who caught all the prawns at dawn?
8. Paul will launch the trawler after the auction.
9. The author saw the law book in the small pouch.
10. Mary left the shawl and blouse at the laundry.

ea from the red code

In the words below, the **ea** has the same sound as the *short* **e** sound in 'red' e .

Box 1

dead
head
lead
bread

Box 2

tread
spread
thread
instead

Box 3

feather
heather
weather
leather

Box 4

health
wealth
breath
death

ea **from the red code**

In the words below, the **ea** has the same sound as the short **e** sound in 'red' e .

Box 5

read
ready
steady
already

Box 6

breast
breakfast
heavy
weapon

Box 7

<u>treasure</u>
<u>measure</u>
<u>pleasure</u>
pleasant

Box 8

deaf
sweat
heaven
earth

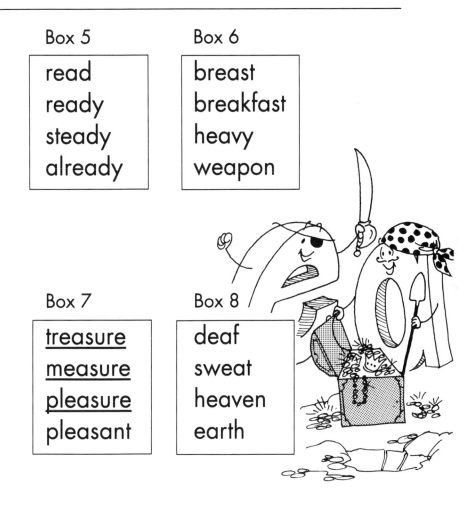

In the words underlined the **s** has a zh sound.

Both of these have the same sound
oi as in oil, boil
oy as in boy, toy

oi

Box 1

oil
boil
toil
soil

Box 2

coil
foil
spoil
toilet

Box 3

join
coin
joint
point

Box 4

moist
hoist
noise
avoid

Box 5

voice
choice
rejoice
poison

 oi

 oy

Both of these have the same sound
oi as in oil, boil
oy as in boy, toy

 oy

Box 1

boy
toy
joy
Moy

Box 2

annoy
employ
enjoy
destroy

Spelling Tip:
When this sound comes at the *end* of a word it is usually spelled **oy**. When it comes in the *middle* of a word it is usually **oi**.

Words where **oy**, is not at the end of a word.

Box 3   loyal   royal   voyage   oyster

Word endings

-ng

-ng

Box 1

sang
rang
bang
fang

Box 2

gang
tang
slang
sprang

Box 3

long
strong
wrong
throng

Box 4

hung
flung
clung
stung

Box 5

ring
king
sing
wing

Box 6

bring
sting
fling
string

Box 7

anything
something
everything
nothing

Box 8

coming
bringing
taking
eating

56

Word endings

-nk

Box 1	Box 2	Box 3	Box 4
bank	shank	blank	Frank
tank	spank	drank	swank
sank	thank	crank	flank
rank	prank	plank	clank

Box 5	Box 6	Box 7	Box 8
hunk	skunk	pink	think
bunk	chunk	wink	blink
junk	drunk	rink	slink
punk	slunk	link	stink

57

Word endings

-nd

-nd	Box 1	Box 2	Box 3	Box 4

Box 1
band
land
sand
hand

Box 2
stand
grand
strand
brand

Box 3
bend
send
lend
mend

Box 4
spend
blend
trend
friend

Box 5
intend
pretend
depend
suspend

Box 6
extend
expand
demand
remand

Box 7
fond
pond
blond
beyond

Box 8
blind
grind
behind
remind

58

Word endings

-nt

Box 1	Box 2	Box 3	Box 4

-nt

Box 1
ant
slant
plant
grant

Box 2
went
lent
spent
cement

Box 3
silent
different
prevent
accident

Box 4
stunt
shunt
blunt
grunt

Box 5
print
flint
sprint
squint

Box 6
amount
account
discount
dismount

Time for a test

1. Remind me to thank the gang you employ.
2. Pat gave a grunt when he sank in the wet cement.
3. Pretend you spent the week on a grand voyage.
4. Oysters have very strong shells.
5. The girl who sang on the band stand had a lovely voice.
6. Let the boy bring the plank to the hoist.
7. Put the plant in different soil behind the bank.
8. Dad put the joint into the tinfoil.
9. The oil might destroy the noisy toy.
10. Lock up all poisons and avoid accidents.

Word endings

-rt

Box 1

chart
start
smart
depart

Box 2

hurt
spurt
blurt
squirt

Box 3

dirt
flirt
shirt
skirt

Box 4

report
deport
import
export

Box 5

desert
dessert
expert
exert

Box 6

heart
impart
restart
support

Word endings

-ft

Box 1

| raft |
| shaft |
| craft |
| graft |

Box 2

| left |
| deft |
| cleft |
| theft |

Box 3

| soft |
| loft |
| gift |
| rift |

Box 4

| lift |
| shift |
| drift |
| swift |

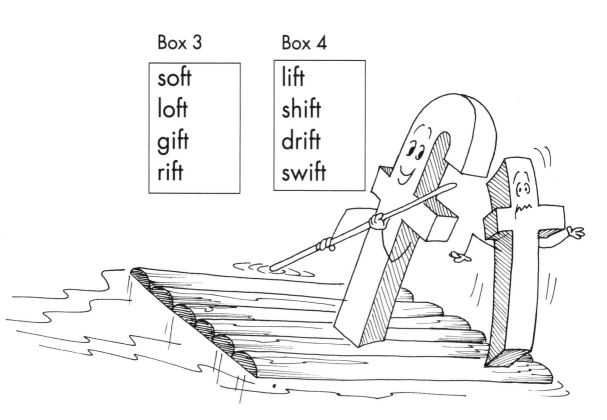

Word endings

-ct

-ct

Box 1

act
fact
tact
intact

Box 2

exact
enact
subtract
contract

Box 3

erect
direct
correct
collect

Box 4

connect
inspect
expect
suspect

Box 5

effect
protect
infect
inject

Box 6

duct
conduct
instruct
product

Box 7

strict
reflect
subject
object

Word endings

-lt

-lt

Box 1

halt
malt
salt
fault

Box 2

belt
felt
built
quilt

Box 3

bolt
colt
jolt
revolt

Box 4

insult
consult
result
exult

Box 5

silt
kilt
wilt
spilt

Word endings -mp

-mp

Box 1

lamp
damp
ramp
stamp

Box 2

cramp
clamp
tramp
scamp

Box 3

swamp
champ
plump
slump

Box 4

pump
jump
lump
rump

Box 5

hump
thump
clump
grump

Box 6

limp
skimp
chimp
shrimp

Word endings

-pt

-pt	Box 1	Box 2	Box 3

Box 1	Box 2	Box 3
kept	accept	erupt
slept	adopt	abrupt
crept	tempt	interrupt
except	attempt	corrupt

Word endings

-tch

Practise
atch, etch, otch, utch and **itch**
before attempting the words below.

	Box 1	Box 2	Box 3	Box 4
-tch	match catch latch batch	hatch patch watch thatch	scratch snatch despatch	fetch ketch sketch stretch

Box 5	Box 6	Box 7	Box 8
hutch Dutch crutch clutch	ditch bitch hitch pitch	witch stitch switch	notch blotch Scotch

Time for a test

1. Fetch the lamp and shift it to the left side of the loft.
2. We will inspect the pitch before the match.
3. Collect the exact amount for the watch.
4. Who will stitch the patch on the tramp's shirt?
5. Connect the switch to the lamp in the shaft.
6. The champ had to use a crutch after the fight.
7. The doctor will inject my arm but I must protect the cut from dirt.
8. We export more than we import.
9. When the teacher corrects my spellings I expect to get a good result.
10. The raft has left the ketch and will drift out to sea.

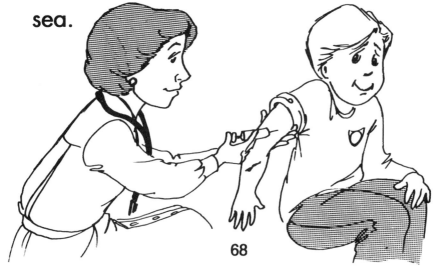

Important points to remember

1. A vowel is usually *short* when it is the only vowel in the word and is followed by a consonant as in –

   met, cot, can, etc.

2. A vowel is usually *long* when it is the only vowel and is the last letter of the word.

   he, me, go, etc.

3. In a *short* word which has two vowels (one of which is silent **e** at the end) the first vowel is long and the **e** keeps quiet –

   take, dime, hope, etc.

4. When two vowels come together in a word, the first is usually long and the second keeps quiet as in –

   coat, nail, seat, etc.

5. **c** has the ⟨s⟩ sound and **g** has the ⟨j⟩ sound when the next letter is **e, i,** or **y** –

   city, rice, fancy, page, fringe

Useful words

Box 1

radio
television
video
programme

Box 2

address
envelope
letter
parcel

Box 3

referee
foul
penalty
goal

Box 4

apples
oranges
pears
peaches

Box 5

potatoes
cabbage
turnips
carrots

Box 6

doctor
examine
prescription
medicine

Useful words

Box 7

question
answer
problem
difficult

Box 8

addition
subtraction
multiply
divide

Box 9

travel
station
ticket
journey

Box 10

weather
forecast
thunder
lightning

Box 11

factory
cinema
museum
supermarket

Box 12

building
roof
ceiling
floor

Anagrams

Anagrams are words where the letters are jumbled. See if you can find out what each word is. The clues will help you.

Clues

orgnts	The opposite of weak.
tyrunec	A hundred years.
rscicu	You might see clowns here.
bacgaeb	A vegetable.
rtineeht	A baker's dozen.
belwo	Part of the arm.
stdyayeer	The day before today.
threaef	As light as a _____ .
nlbut	not sharp.
cawht	This will tell the time.

Find the missing letters

Clues

bl _ _ d	To lose blood.
ch _ _ se	mice love this.
sl _ _ p	What you do at night.
cl _ _ n	The opposite of dirty.
fl _ _ t	A cork would do this in water.
sn _ _ l	He can carry his own house.
w _ _ k	You might feel this way if you were ill.

Find the missing letters

Clues

br _ _ m	Another name for a brush.
s _ _ sons	There are four of them in a year.
s _ _ cer	It is usually seen with a cup.
m _ _ se	'Mice' means more than one of these.
p _ _ se	To stop for a while.
fl _ _ r	Bread is made from this.
sp _ _ n	Rhymes with 'soon'.

Tongue twisters

See how quickly you can read them.

1. The sticky sand was stuck on the steep step at the stable door.

2. I can skate and skip and play skittles with skill.

3. Strong Sam stroked the strip and stuck the strap in the street.

4. Trace the face and place the brace in space.

5. The sick smith smashed the stick with a smack.

6. Soak the black cloak and float the boat in the moat.

Tongue twisters

See how quickly you can read them.

1. Sandy stole the spotted spanner and the studded stopper.
2. The printer got a splinter in his finger in spring.
3. Strap the spring on the string and stick the ring on the spring.
4. The swallow will follow the harrow in the hollow.
5. The ice was twice the price and the mice ate all the rice.
6. The strange ranger changed the range for the stranger.

Find the letters

Find the letters to complete the first word and start the second word. These pairs of letters will help you.

sp, sh, st, ch,

e.g. | pat**ch**arge |

chur _ _ amp

bru _ _ ort

fla _ _ ock

fro _ _ orm

sma _ _ ine

gra _ _ ark

snat _ _ eck

spla _ _ elf

cre _ _ ruck

stit _ _ ange

You may use the same pair more than once.

Find the letters

Find the letters to complete the first word and start the second word. These pairs of letters will help you.

sp, sh, st, ch, th, sk

stret _ _ est

whi _ _ ubby

clo _ _ umb

thru _ _ out

cri _ _ ank

swit _ _ unk

flu _ _ aft

smoo _ _ eft

fri _ _ ate

bran _ _ ess

You may use the same pair more than once.

Silly words

Here are some silly words, which don't make any sense. See if you can read them.

stoft	spouch
spronk	flooch
shrump	spland
splong	blonk
strept	flimps
clotch	chirgop
prumpt	scrubnib
grong	brimpmop
shramp	vilpod
prunk	dumdup

Why not try to invent your own 'silly words'? Make a list.